A Compendium of Ways of Knowing

A Compendium of Ways of Knowing

A Clear Mirror of what should be Accepted and Rejected

("Blo-rigs-kyi sdom-tsig blang-dor gsal-ba'i me-long")

by
A-kya Yong-dzin Yang-chän ga-wäi lo-dr'ö

With commentary compiled from oral teachings by
Geshe Ngawang Dhargyey

Translated and edited by
Sherpa Tulku and Alexander Berzin
with
Khamlung Tulku and Jonathan Landaw

LIBRARY OF TIBETAN WORKS AND ARCHIVES

ISBN: 81-85102-12-0

Published by the Library of Tibetan Works and Archives, Dharamsala 176215, India, and printed at Indraprastha Press (CBT), Nehru House, New Delhi-110002.

Contents

Publisher's Note

As part of its expanding educational program, the Library of Tibetan Works and Archives has undertaken the preparation of graded textbooks on various topics. In 1976 the first edition of *A Compendium of Ways of Knowing* was published. The present volume is the third edition of this work and is an introduction to the subject matter of ways of knowing studied in the second class of the standard Tibetan Buddhist curriculum as taught in the Ge-lug lineage.

It is hoped that in publishing such graded textbooks as this, the Library can help provide the study materials for establishing the Tibetan Buddhist educational system in foreign languages.

Gyatsho Tshering
Director

April 1996

Preface

Among the Tibetans, the Buddhist monasteries have traditionally been great centres of learning. The educational system followed in many of them, such as Ga-dän, Se-ra and Drä-pung of the Ge-lug tradition, is modelled on that introduced from India more than a thousand years ago. Each of these monastic centres is divided into several monasteries composed of many small schools. Each monastery has its own set of textbooks, but the education is uniform throughout. Upon its successful completion, monks are awarded the Geshe degree, for which they must be at least twenty-five years of age. Similar systems of study can be found in many monasteries of the other Tibetan lineages of Buddhism as well, with slight variation in curriculum, degree requirements and titles conferred.

The novices begin their formal studies at about the age of eight, after they have been taught to read and write. Very quickly they begin to memorize the major texts that will form the basis of their later studies. These texts have been translated from Sanskrit and only after they have been fully memorized will they be explained. Although in their classes the novices receive lectures, the main emphasis in the Ge-lug tradition is on debating. Having had a point explained to them, the students pair off to explore with each other its implications, defence and possible refutation. This ensures that they understand what they are taught and do not merely accept things as true without knowing why.

The topic of the first class is called definitions (Dü-ra)s. In it the young novices learn the fundamentals of debating. Memorizing a large number of formal definitions, they develop their powers of reasoning by debating on such topics as cause and effect, existents and non-existents, positive and negative phenomena, sets and sub-sets, and mutual exclusion and lines of reasoning. At the conclusion of this course, at about the age of nine or ten, they enter the second class, which is on ways of knowing (Lo-rig). A synopsis of this subject is given in the present text. The third class deals with ways of reasoning (Tag-rig).

Having completed these three preparatory classes, the novices are ready to begin the five primary subjects for the Geshe degree, the major texts for which they have already memorized. First they learn the perfection of discriminating awareness (prajñāpāramitā), then the middle way (mādhyamaka), validities (pramāna), laws (vinaya) and finally general knowledge (abhidharma). The perfection of discriminating awareness is the study of the hidden meaning of the Voidness teachings within the widespread action teachings of the Enlightened Motive of Bodhicitta. It also deals specifically with the stages and paths to Enlightenment, and is based on *A Filigree of What to Realize (Abhisamayālaṁkara)* by Maitreya. The middle way is the study of the profound insight teachings of Voidness and the ten perfections, based on *A Supplement to (Nāgārjuna's) 'Treatise on the Middle Way' (Mādhyamakāvatāra)* by Candrakīrti. Validities is the study of logic, of the mind and theory of learning, based on *A Commentary to (Dignāga's 'Compendium of) Validities' (Pramāṇavarttika)* by Dharmakīrti. Laws is the study of disciplinary vows and the law of cause and effect, based on *The Sūtra of Laws (Vinayasūtra)* by Gunaprabha. General knowledge is the study of metaphysics and cosmology, based on *A Treasury of General Knowledge (Abhidharmakośa)* by Vasubandhu.

The following text, written in the late eighteenth century, is from the second preliminary class, concerning ways of knowing. It is found in *The Collected Works of A-kya Yoṅs-ḥdzin*, vol. 1 (New Delhi: Lama Guru Deva, 1971), folios 515-526. It is a compendium of the major points of this subject, written in metered verse similar to jingles. Phrases inserted to fill out the meaning in the English translation have been indicated by their inclusion within parentheses. This is a sample of the type of text memorized by young novices in this class so that they will have the most important definitions and lists of divisions clear in their minds for use in debate. The explanation follows the set of textbooks written by Je-tzün Ch'ö-kyi gyäl-tsän, used in the colleges of Se-ra J'e and Ga-dän J'ang-tze monasteries. It has been compiled and translated here by Sherpa Tulku and Alexander Berzin, with the assistance of Khamlung Tulku and Jonathan Landaw, from several oral discourses given by Geshe Ngawang Dhargyey at the Library of Tibetan Works and Archives in Dharamsala, India. It is printed here in indented format. The compilers have also consulted with Tsenshap Serkong Rinpoche, L.T. Doboom Tulku and Alan Wallace. The second edition has been prepared and the root text retranslated by Alexander Berzin based on further clarification and revision received from Geshe Ngawang Dhargyey, Geshe Sonam Rinchen, Geshe Dawa and Yeshe Lodro

Rinpoche. The kind and patient assistance of all these participants in this project is gratefully acknowledged.

The textbooks of the various monasteries explain the subjects from slightly different points of view. This is purposeful and in keeping with the Buddha's general method of teaching with skilful means. The main objective of the monastic educational system is to prepare young novices to think for themselves and develop their mind to its fullest potential. This is all for the purpose of achieving the Omniscience of the Full Enlightenment of Buddhahood in order to be able to help all sentient beings. If a subject, such as ways of knowing, were to be presented in a dogmatic fashion with but one orthodox interpretation, this would leave little room for the students' mental development and creativity. But with each monastery using different textbooks having alternative explanations, the debates between their students become more lively and challenging. In this way the novices learn to become great teachers themselves, making rapid progress along the pathway to Enlightenment. Therefore, although alternative explanations of several minor points concerning ways of knowing may be found in various texts, yet if the ultimate purpose of the study of this subject is kept in mind, one will remain unconfused and undaunted, ever focused and stimulated towards the goal.

1

Introductory Discussion

Homage to Mañjuśri.

This text concerns the mind and the ways in which it knows things. By understanding how your mind works and training it properly, you can attain Omniscience and the Full Enlightenment of Buddhahood. You will then be able to liberate from their suffering all sentient beings, that is everyone else with a mind. Homage is therefore made to Mañjuśri who manifests the complete wisdom of the Buddhas.

As people have different levels of aptitude, Buddha has taught many different schools of theories to meet their needs. This text is written from the Sautrāntika point of view. According to it all things validly knowable, that is validly cognizable, are either impermanent or permanent depending on whether or not they have the ability to produce an effect. There are three kinds of impermanent phenomena: those with physical qualities, those with qualities of consciousness and those with neither. The first category has ten divisions: sights, sounds, smells, tastes, bodily sensations, plus the physical cognitive sensors of the sensors corresponding to each of them. The second, phenomena having qualities of consciousness, has three divisions: primary consciousness, secondary mental factors and awareness of consciousness. Impermanent phenomena having neither physical qualities nor those of consciousness include instincts, all sentient beings' person or conventional "I" and so forth.

Something having qualities of consciousness is defined as an impermanent phenomenon of a clear awareness involved with an object. With primary consciousness you are aware merely of the fundamental data of a sight, sound and so forth. With secondary mental factors, you become aware of distinctions in such objects, make judgements about them, react to them and so forth.

With awareness of consciousness you know that you have been conscious of something and you experience this in the sense of witnessing it.

Take the example of seeing a beautiful work of art. With the first type of consciousness you receive its bare visual impression. With the second you identify it as a work of art, judge it to be beautiful, react to it with pleasure and so on. With the third you are aware of your state of mind.

A consciousness in general is defined as a principal faculty of awareness upon which can be placed the impression of the fundamental data of anything that can be validly cognized. Thus consciousness refers specifically to primary consciousness, and there are six types in connection with the six cognitive sensors. Visual consciousness depends on the physical eye-sensors to become aware of sights or forms; audial on those of the ears for sounds; olfactory on those of the nose for smells; gustatory on those of the tongue for tastes, and tactile on those of the body for sensations of touch. Mental consciousness depends on the non-physical mental sensors to become aware of anything validly knowable.

The objects and sensors of each cognitive faculty, such as that of vision, are known as its sources, and thus there are twelve cognitive bases. When the consciousness of that faculty is added to its objects and cognitive sensors, they are called the three spheres of that faculty, and of these there are eighteen. When a moment of consciousness of a particular faculty, its attendant secondary mental factors and awareness of consciousness are grouped together, they are known as conscious phenomena of that faculty or as an instance of its cognition.

Thus there are the cognitive faculties of seeing, hearing, smelling, tasting, touching and thinking. Encompassing all six is your faculty of knowing. Through it you know things or have knowledge of them in a variety of ways. As this faculty is an impermanent phenomenon and since such things are defined as the ability to produce an effect, then in fact what is discussed are the various everchanging instances of the functioning of this faculty, that is specific instances of various ways of knowing things. To simplify the language of this translation, "the faculty of knowing", "knowledge", "knowing", and "ways of knowing" are often used interchangeably.

An explanation of the systems of ways of knowing involves both knowledge, which is something that has an object, and also its objects. In general, things that have objects are defined as any functional phenomenon that (continually) possesses or takes some object appropriate to itself. Such things may be phenomena having either physical qualities, those of consciousness or non-associated compositional factors. An example of the first is all communicating sounds, of the second every cognition, and of the third everyone's person or conventional "I".

> All spoken words *signify* something. Cognitions are always *of* something and a conventional "I" must *refer to* someone. Thus each of these types of impermanent phenomena is always in conjunction with a specific object. Thus they are things that have objects.

There are definitions, synonyms and divisions of knowing. As for the first of these, the defining characteristic of a way of knowing is awareness. Knowing, cognizing, being aware of and having a clear experience of something are all mutually inclusive terms.

> For two terms, "x" and "y", to be mutually inclusive they must satisfy the eight requirements of congruence: if it is "x" it is "y" and if it is "y" it is "x"; if it is not "x" it is not "y" and if it is not "y" it is not "x"; if there is an "x" there is a "y" and if there is a "y" there is an "x"; and if there is no "x" there is no "y" and if there is no "y" there is no "x". Thus if you know something you are aware of it, if you do not know something you are unaware of it, and so forth. The standard example is that if something is impermanent it is the product of causes.
>
> An example of two terms that are not mutually inclusive is a vase and being impermanent. Although if something is a vase it must be impermanent, it is not the case that if it is impermanent it must be a vase, or if not a vase it must be permanent.
>
> The relation, then, between these two is one of pervasion. "x" is pervasive with "y" if all instances of "x" are "y", although all "y" need not be "x". All vases are

impermanent, but not all impermanent things are not vases.

When (ways of knowing are) divided there are many aspects. You can know something either with or without apprehending it. Moreover you can know it in seven different ways. In addition there are both valid and invalid ways of knowing, as well as conceptual and non-conceptual ones. There are bare perceptions and inferential understandings, primary consciousness and secondary mental factors and many such things.

A way of knowing something is said to be either with or without apprehension depending on whether or not it apprehends its own object.

> When one of your types of consciousness apprehends something, this does not mean that it necessarily comprehends or understands what it is. It merely means that it has taken its object correctly and decisively so that later you will have no doubts. If you see a white snow mountain as white, you have apprehended it correctly. If you see it as yellow, you have not.

Of the seven ways of knowing, you can apprehend things through bare perception, inference or subsequent cognition. With the other four you know something, but you have not apprehended it.

> Thus if your knowledge of something is presumptive, inattentive, indecisive or distorted, you have not apprehended it correctly or decisively.

The statement by some scholars that presumption is a way of knowing something with apprehension should be taken in the sense that with presumption you can just about apprehend something.

You may apprehend something either directly or indirectly. This is determined by whether or not an aspect of the object you apprehend actually dawns on your consciousness.

> When you have a bare visual perception of something blue, for instance, you have a direct apprehension of what is blue and an indirect one of what is not blue. When you hear a man speaking in the next room, you directly apprehend the sound of his voice. Although his form does not actually dawn on your visual consciousness, you know indirectly that he is there.

From *The Elimination of Mental Darkness Concerning (Dharmakīrti's) Seven Treatises (on Validities)* (by K'ä-drup Je): "It is said that (1) in general, valid ways of knowing can be direct and indirect; and (2) with bare perception and inference you may have direct and indirect apprehension. The first statement is a very rough one, while the second is the Sautrāntika position. Or the latter could be taken in the sense that both (types of apprehension may occur) in specific instances of bare perception and inference."

> Thus to say that valid ways of knowing, that is bare perception and inference, can apprehend objects both directly and indirectly, is only a rough general statement. It does not mean that every instance of them does so. Any specific instance of these valid ways of knowing can apprehend objects either only directly or both directly and indirectly. This is how the Sautrāntikas explain this topic.

"As for how an invalid way of knowing something can nevertheless correctly apprehend its object directly or indirectly, this should be understood in the same way as explained for the valid ones."

> A valid way of knowing something is defined as a fresh, non-fraudulent awareness of it. To say that your knowledge must be fresh in order to be valid precludes the possibility of subsequent cognition being considered a valid means of knowing. Since it must be non-fraudulent, presumption cannot be taken as valid, and since it must be an awareness, the physical cognitive sensors such as the photosensitive cells of the eyes, for instance, cannot be considered as such either.
>
> Even though subsequent cognition is invalid because it is not fresh, this does not mean that it is fraudulent. Once you have initially inferred or have had a bare perception of an object and thus have apprehended it correctly and decisively, your subsequent cognition of it continues to discern it this way. Therefore, in the same manner as these two valid ways of knowing, it too can apprehend objects both directly and indirectly or only directly.

The seven ways of knowing something are by presumption, inattentive perception, subsequent cognition, distorted cognition, indecisive wavering, bare perception and inferential understanding.

Of these seven only the last two are valid. Subsequent cognition, bare perception and inferential understanding, however, each apprehend their objects. Distorted cognition is the worst of all since it falsifies what is correct.

2

Presumption

Presumption is defined as an invalid way of knowing that (takes) its object correctly and conceptually cognizes it freshly.

Through a valid means such as inference you have a fresh, conceptual understanding of a correct conclusion. Here, however, you have a fresh reaching of a correct conclusion without really understanding it or knowing why it is true. With presumption, therefore, you merely seem to understand or apprehend something freshly, because what you know is true, but actually your knowledge of it is indecisive and invalid. You presume it to be true either for no reason, a wrong one, or even a right one but without understanding why it is correct.

There are five kinds of presumption: presuming what is true to be so (1) for no reason, (2) for a contradictory reason, (3) for a non-determining one, (4) for an irrelevant one and (5) for a correct reason, but without any decisiveness. Examples of each in turn are said to be as follows. (The first is) the knowledge assuming that sound changes (when you reach this conclusion) by merely (hearing) the words, "Sound is a changing phenomenon." When to prove this you use lines of reasoning that are contradictory, non-determining or irrelevant, or when you rely on a (correct) reason—(because it is) a product of causes—(but are not yet convinced that this proves anything), these are the examples of the other types of presumption by which you can also assume that sound changes.

To understand something by inference depends on a correct line of reasoning. This involves the use of a three-part logical demonstration such as sound is impermanent because it is the product of causes. This is one of the most commonly used examples in Buddhist logic since it is used to refute the assertion by several non-Buddhist schools that such sounds as the words of certain sacred scriptures are eternal and permanent because they are the revelations of super-empirical truths without any author.

In this case sound is the subject or the basis of the proposition. Being impermanent is what is to be proved about it. These two together are known as the thesis—sound is impermanent. Because it is the product of causes is the line of reasoning or simply the reason used to prove it. The opposite of what is to be proved, in this case being permanent, is what is to be disproved. This and the subject of the proposition taken together form the antithesis—sound is permanent. Everything to which what is to be proved applies—all impermanent phenomena—constitutes the analogous set. Everything to which the opposite applies—all permanent phenomena—constitutes the counter-set.

To prove a thesis and disprove its antithesis, then, three factors must be established about the line of reasoning: (1) the reason must pertain to or be a property of the subject of the proposition; (2) it must be an exclusive characteristic of the analogous set and (3) it must be a quality never found in the counter-set. These three are known as the factors of agreement, congruence and incongruence.

In the logical demonstration that sound is impermanent because it is a product of causes, the reason—being a product of causes—is (1) a property of sound, (2) an exclusive characteristic of all impermanent phenomena and (3) never a quality of things that are permanent. Thus because (1) sound is a product of causes, (2) impermanent phenomena are the only things that are products and (3) there are no permanent things that are products, you correctly conclude that sound is impermanent with a full and decisive understanding of how and why. This is an example of an inferential understanding, a valid way of knowing something to be true that is not obvious by relying on validating reasons.

With presumption, on the other hand, because there is some fault in your line of reasoning you can only presume something to be true, for you do not fully understand why. The last four types of presumption are illustrated as follows.

You conclude that sound is impermanent because you believe it to be non-functional. If something is non-functional, it is not a product of causes and does not produce any effects. This, however, is the Sautrāntika definition of permanent phenomena such as space, defined as the absence of anything tangible that impedes motion. The empty space or place that a physical thing occupies does not in any way affect it. Nor is this space created when you remove the object; it was there all the' time. Thus it is permanent because it is non-functional. To conclude, however, that sound is impermanent because it is not functional is contradictory to the facts. Examine the three factors. (1) Does being non-functional apply to sound? No, it does not. If you hear a loud noise you may be startled. (2) Is it an exclusive characteristic of the analogous set? On the contrary, there is not one impermanent phenomenon that does not produce an effect, for this is the definition of impermanence. (3) Is it a quality never found among those things in the counter-set? It is not, for all permanent phenomena are defined as being non-functional. Therefore to conclude that sound is impermanent because it is non-functional is a presumption based on a contradictory reason.

You may reach this same conclusion by using the line of reason: because it is something that can be validly known. (1) Can sound be validly known? Yes, it can. This reason satisfies the factor of agreement with the subject of the proposition. (2) Is being validly knowable an exclusive characteristic of the analogous set? On the one hand it is true that all impermanent phenomena may be validly known, but on the other hand everything that can be validly known is not necessarily impermanent. Both permanent and impermanent phenomena can be known in this way. Therefore this fails that test of congruence. (3) Is being validly knowable a quality that never applies to anything in the counter-set? No, everything permanent may be validly known. Therefore this reason fails the test of incongruence as well. Thus to conclude that sound is impermanent because it can be validly known is presumption based on a non-determining reason.

You may also conclude correctly as above, but for the reason that it is something that can be seen by the eye. Being visible, however, (1) is not a quality of sound, (2) is not an exclusive quality of impermanent phenomena and (3) is not a quality never found among those things that are permanent. Everything impermanent is not necessarily visible and some permanent phenomena such as an empty space may be seen indirectly. Therefore to reach the correct conclusion that sound is impermanent because it may be seen by the eye is presumption based on an irrelevant reason.

A correct line of reasoning for concluding that sound is impermanent is because it is a product of causes. However, if you reach this correct conclusion and say it is for this reason, but do not understand what being the product of causes means or what it has to do with being impermanent, then you have presumed what is true to be so for a correct reason, but without any decisiveness.

These (five) may be condensed into two categories: the first is presumption based on no reason, while the latter four have some reason (that is either incorrect or, if correct, not understood). Most of the understanding you gain from merely hearing something is presumptive knowledge. Therefore it is said that the stream of continuity of such knowledge is unstable.

Knowledge may be gained from either hearing, contemplating or meditating. When you merely hear or read a fact, however, if you do not think about it or examine it carefully to understand how and why it is true, you usually can only presume it to be so. Because you have not comprehended it fully, often you cannot remember such factual knowledge. Thus it is said that its stream of continuity is unsteady because often such knowledge does not endure. Another example is uncritical faith, which is a form of respectful belief based on no reason.

3

Inattentive Perception

Inattentive perception is a way of knowing an involved object when (that object) is an objective entity that appears clearly (to one of your types of consciousnesses), yet you are inattentive of it. There are three varieties: (1) bare sensory and (2) bare mental perception and (3) the bare perception of awareness of consciousness, when any of these has become (inattentive).

> In general there are four kinds of bare perception: sensory, mental, that of awareness of consciousness and yogic. With these you may know objective entities as the objects involved. When through a non-defective sense organ one of your five sensory types of consciousness apprehends an object freshly and correctly, without mixing it with any conceptualizations or ideas, this is bare sensory perception. An example is the first moment of your visual consciousness correctly perceiving the form of a vase. After having such a bare sensory perception and before your mind begins to conceptualize about it, your mental consciousness must first also take the form of this vase correctly. This is the bare mental perception of a form. It lasts only a very short time. Your initial awareness of such valid cognitions, which allows you to later remember them, is the bare perception of awareness of consciousness. When you have had such bare perceptions, yet are unsure of them or your attention is preoccupied, these are then termed inattentive.

There is no such thing as inattentive yogic perception, since everything that appears (to it)·is paid (full) attention.

> Every sentient being consists of five aggregate physical and mental faculties. All the physical objects of cognition, including his body and its physical cognitive sensors, constitute his aggregate of form. His aggregate of consciousness is his six types of primary consciousness,

while his aggregate of recognition and response or feeling are his secondary mental factors performing these two functions. All his other secondary mental factors, as well as his instincts, his conventional "I" or person and all other such impermanent phenomena lacking either physical qualities or those of consciousness, are grouped together as his aggregate compositional factors. Thus this fifth aggregate includes everything else composing his cognition that is impermanent and not found in his other four aggregates. His conventional "I" is the point of reference by which he is known. It accounts for how he and others can label the name "I" or any name onto his particular collection of aggregate physical and mental faculties.

In the Sautrāntika theories Buddha explained that everyone does have a valid conventional "I". However, such an impermanent phenomenon lacks an identity that is (1) permanent, singular and independent from the ever-changing five aggregates for which it is a convenient label, and (2) self-sufficiently and substantially existent as a master of the aggregates. These are known respectively as the coarse and subtle Identitylessness of the conventional "I" or person.

Anyone having a non-conceptual correct apprehension of either of these is called a Noble One or an Ārya. Such a being has in his meditation achieved a union or yoga of mental quiescence and penetrative insight. The former is an exhilarating state of consciousness free from all conceptualizations as well as any mental dullness, agitation or wandering. The latter is a correct apprehension of either subtle impermanence or the coarse or subtle Identitylessness of the conventional "I". In his meditation on Identitylessness, then, an Ārya has bare perception directly apprehending the impermanence of his aggregates, the conventional "I" of which is devoid of a permanent or substantially existing identity. In this way he indirectly apprehends the Identitylessness of his conventional "I". This is known as bare yogic perception and, according to the Sautrāntika explanation, it is experienced only by Āryas.

There are five kinds of bare sensory perception of this type. These would be like, for instance, an ordinary being's five types of bare sensory perception, from that taking a form through to that taking a bodily sensation as its object, when his mind is diverted in another direction.

> When you are attentively listening to music, you have bare audial perception of its sound. At such a time your sensory perceptions of the picture on the wall in front of you, of the smell or taste of your cigarette and the feel of your watch on your wrist are all inattentive. Although each of these sensory objects appears clearly to your visual consciousness, your olfactory and so forth, you cannot be certain that they are there. You take no notice of them because your attention is preoccupied, that is diverted elsewhere.

Or (another example would be) the final moment (in a particular stream of continuity) of any of the five kinds of sensory perception in an ordinary being's mindstream.

> When, for instance, as an ordinary being with non-defective senses, you correctly see a vase, your visual perception of it free of any conceptualization may last for several moments. The first instant when your knowledge is fresh is your bare perception of the vase, and this is a valid knowing of it. Afterwards, although you still apprehend the vase correctly, your knowledge of it is no longer fresh and thus your subsequent cognition is invalid. During the last instant of the stream of continuity of this particular sense perception, however, you no longer even apprehend the vase correctly. Your attention is about to shift to another object and, like a candle about to go out, your clarity becomes very dim. Although the vase still appears to your visual consciousness, you are not paying full attention to it. This final moment is an example of inattentive visual perception.

The tiniest moment of bare mental perception and all (such tiniest moments of) the awareness of consciousness of ordinary beings are inattentive perceptions. However, the type of bare mental perception indicated here, when it is of an Ārya, is valid. This is attested to in *The Filigrœ of (Valid) Lines of Reasoning* (by His Holiness the First Dalai Lama).

Unlike Buddhas, the lower Āryas do not continue to have joint mental quiescence and penetrative insight after they leave their meditation on Identitylessness. They have bare yogic perception only during such a meditation period, and this is never inattentive. Even during their post-meditational periods, however, every tiniest moment of their bare mental perception and that of their awareness of consciousness is never inattentive. This is not the case with ordinary beings. The tiniest moment of bare mental perception that follows a stream of continuity of their bare sensory perception is too quick to be attentive. Likewise, although their bare perception of awareness of consciousness can be attentive, this attention requires several moments to be established. Therefore its tiniest moments by themselves are inattentive.

Bare perceptions of awareness of consciousness of this (inattentive) type (also) include, for instance, those experiencing valid inferential understandings in the mindstreams of Cārvākas and Jains, those experiencing distorted perceptions and so forth. (All bare perceptions of) the awareness of consciousness in the mindstreams of Vaibhāṣika Buddhists and the final moment of any stream of continuity of an ordinary being's awareness of consciousness (are also inattentive). There are many such examples.

According to the theories of the Cārvākas and the Jains, you cannot know anything validly by inferential understanding. Nevertheless, when adherents of these two non-Buddhist schools see smoke on a mountain, they know there is fire. Although such valid inferential understanding appears clearly in their mindstream, and although their awareness of consciousness actually experiences this inference, they are not fully aware of it. This is because their mind is preoccupied with their belief that there is no such thing as inference. Thus this perception of their awareness of consciousness is inattentive.

Likewise, when you have a distorted perception, such as of a blue snow mountain, and an image of one appears clearly to your visual consciousness—although in fact there is no such thing—your awareness of this perception is also inattentive. Except for that of an Ārya, an ordinary being's awareness of consciousness merely experiences or is aware of a mental state or cognition. It does not understand what this cognition is of or whether or not it is correct. Thus with your awareness of consciousness you merely experience a distorted perception without knowing it is incorrect. However, because your mind is preoccupied with thinking that what you see is truly so, you are not fully aware of your distorted perception. Therefore the cognition of this distorted perception by your awareness of consciousness is inattentive.

When Buddha taught the Vaibhāṣika theories, he did not explain that sentient beings have a mental faculty of awareness of consciousness. Although adherents of this belief experience their mental states and cognitions through such a faculty, they are not fully aware of it. This is because their mind is preoccupied with their misconception that they have no such faculty. All such perceptions in their mindstream of awareness of consciousness, therefore, are also inattentive.

4

Subsequent Cognition

Subsequent cognition is defined as an invalid awareness which apprehends what has already been apprehended. There are three types: those that arise in a stream of continuity following from (1) a (valid) bare perception, (2) a (valid) inferential understanding and (3) those that are in neither of these two (categories).

Both permanent and impermanent phenomena may be known validly, the former directly through inferential understanding and the latter directly through bare perception. Although in general impermanent phenomena change from moment to moment, nevertheless according to the Sautrāntika explanation they still exist objectively from their own individual stance. Thus once you have apprehended a vase correctly you can subsequently do so again, for although the impermanent vase has changed from moment to moment there is still objectively a vase existing as an external object that can repeatedly be seen correctly.

Your perception of this vase may last several moments and thus it can be said to have an unbroken stream of continuity. Initially you see it with bare perception. As a fresh, non-fraudulent awareness of it, apprehending the vase correctly and decisively, this is a valid way of knowing it. As this vase changes from moment to moment, so does your cognition of it. You may continue to apprehend it correctly, but normally only the first instance of your doing so is valid. This is because only this initial cognition is a fresh awareness.

During the unbroken stream of continuity of your awareness of this vase, each subsequent moment of cognition depends on the immediately preceding one of the same object as the immediate condition for its clarity and apprehension. The initial moment in such a sequence, however, has no such dependency. It is clear about this object and apprehends it by its own power and thus only it is truly valid according to the Sautrāntika explanation. Each moment in a Buddha's perception, however, is fresh and valid, without ever relying on the immediately preceding one for the power to apprehend its object. But for all other beings, including Āryas, each stream of continuity of a cognition having an initial moment that is fresh and has already been apprehended correctly continues to be so, but through an objectively non-fresh and therefore invalid way of knowing it. Such moments are known as subsequent cognitions.

There are many kinds of subsequent bare perceptions, such as sensory, mental, that of awareness of consciousness and yogic. Examples of each progressively are the second phase (in the stream of continuity following from a specific valid instance) and (1) any of the five bare sensory perceptions, (2) a bare extrasensory (mental) perception cognizing someone else's thoughts, (3) the bare perception of an awareness of consciousness having continuity and (4) a bare yogic perception of an Ārya still training for perfection. The second phase (in the stream of continuity following) from a (valid) bare perception is accepted as a subsequent bare perception not (specifically) in any of these four categories.

The second type (a subsequent cognition of an inferential understanding) is, for instance, the second phase after a fresh and valid inference. As for the third (a subsequent cognition that is neither of a bare perception nor an inferential understanding), this would be, for instance, a cognition with which you are (once more) attentive of something and which was induced by either a specific (previous valid) bare perception or inferential understanding (of that object). (Another example is) the second moment (in the stream of continuity following) from a valid way of knowing.

In this third category are all cognitions of remembering something you have validly known before through either bare perception or inference, including their first moment.

In short, (all these varieties of) subsequent cognition may be condensed into two sorts, conceptual and non-conceptual. Bare perception and inferential understanding are non-conceptual and conceptual respectively. Therefore subsequent cognition of the former is likewise non-conceptual, while that of the latter is conceptual.

5

Distorted Cognition

Distorted cognition is defined as a way of knowing that takes its own object incorrectly.

Of the five invalid ways of knowing things, inattentive perception and subsequent cognition are not necessarily detrimental to your spiritual progress. The former may lead to a correct and valid cognition and the latter may follow one. For instance, the last moment of your conceptual understanding of Identitylessness before you have bare yogic perception of it is inattentive, yet leads directly to this beneficial state of mind. Your subsequent yogic perception of Identitylessness, though invalid since not fresh, nevertheless leads to your full acquaintance with this true way in which all things exist. By developing such familiarity with this correct apprehension in meditation, you will be able when becoming a Buddha to have valid bare perception of it at all times.

Distorted cognition, however, is extremely detrimental to your development. Nevertheless it can have a last instance. If the proper opponents are applied, all such cognitions can be destroyed. A true practitioner feels that delusions and distortions are much easier to overcome than external enemies. This is because he realizes that neither bombs nor sophisticated weapons are needed to root them out. By developing the proper opponents in his mindstream, he can be free of all such obstacles to his Enlightenment.

When subdivided, there are both conceptual and non-conceptual distorted cognition. The former is defined as a conceptual awareness that is deceived with respect to the object about which it conceptualizes. The definition of a non-conceptual distorted cognition is an awareness that is deceived with respect to the object it takes, which (nevertheless) appears clearly (to it). Examples of the first are the two types of grasping at identities, namely of phenomena and persons, while the second is, for instance, like the sensory cognition to which a snow mountain appears to be blue.

All types of conceptual cognition are deceptive in that a mental image is confused with an actual object. Not all are distorted. The appearing object to such a cognition is a mental image. What this mental image is of is known as its conceptualized-about object. In the case of a non-distorted conceptual cognition, such as one of Tibet, for instance, the mental picture you have of this land is the appearing object to your consciousness, while Tibet itself is its conceptualized-about object. Although your idea of what Tibet is like is not the same as the country itself, nevertheless Tibet is something validly knowable.

In a distorted conceptual cognition, however, such as that of the permanent identity of your conventional "I", your mental image of such an identity is the appearing object to your consciousness, while this permanent identity itself would be the conceptualized-about object. But, since your conventional "I" has no such thing as an actual permanent identity, this conceptual cognition is deceived with respect to what it conceptualizes about. As such an object does not exist, any conceptual cognition in which a mental image of one appears is distorted.

When you see a white snow mountain as blue, such as through a haze at a great distance or when wearing tinted glasses, or when you see two moons, by looking at the real one cross-eyed, such objects appear clearly to your consciousness. They are not mixed with any mental images. But your non-conceptual cognition of them is distorted. What appear to your consciousnesses as if they were actual external objects do not, in reality, exist at all. Your consciousness is approaching such seeming objects in a manner that is deceptive and therefore your cognition is distorted.

In *The Elimination of Mental Darkness Concerning Validities* (by K'ädr'ub Je), it says: "Distorted conceptual cognition, conceptual distorted cognition and interpolation are all mutually inclusive. An indecisive wavering not inclined towards fact is also a conceptual distorted cognition."

6

Indecisive Wavering

Indecisive wavering is a secondary mental factor that wonders about two conclusions concerning its object. There are three (varieties): that which is (1) inclined towards fact, (2) not inclined towards fact and (3) that which is evenly balanced (between the two). Examples of each in turn are ways of knowing with which you think (1) "could sound be something that changes", (2) "could sound be static" and (3) "could sound be either static or changing"

Concerning indecisive wavering (some) assert that any form of it is pervasive with being a root delusion. There are also (others) who differentiate between two kinds, that which has delusion (with it) and that which does not.

It is this latter tradition that is commonly followed. Thus an indecisive wavering inclined towards a correct conclusion is not considered a delusion, while those that are inclined towards an incorrect one or are evenly balanced are taken as deluded. A delusion, or moral and mental defilement, is defined as any state of mind that when developed brings about uneasiness and suffering. The six root ones are desire, anger, pride, ignorance, deluded indecisive wavering and the speculative delusions.

7

Bare Perception

The ways of knowing that take as their appearing object objective entities and metaphysical entities are respectively bare perception and conceptual cognition.

According to the Sautrāntika explanation all validly knowable things are either objective or metaphysical entities. The former are impermanent. They arise collected from, that is dependent on being a product of, causes and circumstances and they have the ability to produce an effect. The latter are all permanent. They arise uncollected from, that is without being a product of, causes and circumstances and they have no ability to produce an effect. Objective entities exist objectively or substantially from their own individual stance. On the other hand, metaphysical entities do not exist objectively, yet they do exist in as much as they can be known by a conceptual cognition through a mental label.

Included among objective entities are all impermanent phenomena, that is those having physical qualities, those having qualities of consciousness and those having neither such qualities. As ultimate truths they do not exist merely as that which can be designated by words. They must be directly perceived and personally experienced in order to be known with full clarity. You cannot describe in words to someone the difference between the sweetness of sugar and that of chocolate. He can only know it by tasting it directly himself. The same is true of the pleasure and pain of giving birth and what it is like to have suicidal tendencies or the latent talents of a genius. These are all validly knowable objective entities. When they are the appearing object to one of your types of consciousness, you know them through bare perception.

What exists only in as much as they can be designated by words, then, are metaphysical entities. Because they are known through verbal conventions, they are called conventional truths. For example, if you have ever given birth, you have a firm idea of what it feels like based on understanding and personal experience. Even if you have never experienced it yourself, you may have a flimsy idea of what it is like based on mere sounds or hearsay. You can describe this to someone and then he too will have his own idea. But what has been talked about and come to be known in this case is merely a verbal approximation. It is only an idea of what the experience of giving birth is like, not the actual experience itself. Such an idea is a metaphysical entity and when it appears to your consciousness you know it through a conceptual cognition. The actual experience of giving birth, on the other hand, is an objective entity and can only be known directly through bare perception.

Metaphysical entities such as ideas, then, are permanent in the sense that they are uncollected phenomena incapable of producing any effect. When a woman tells you what it is like to give birth, an idea arises in your mindstream. Her telling you is the occasion that marks this arisal, but unlike actually giving birth, your idea was not the result of a long process of cause and effect. It was not conceived and nurtured over a period of nine months and did not require a special diet and rest nor the help of nurses and doctors. It was not collected by any accumulation of causes and circumstances, it merely came about uncollected, as it were. Moreover, your idea of giving birth is incapable of producing any effect. It does not make you exhausted or your muscles ache, nor does it produce something that needs to be fed or have its dirty clothes changed. When this idea is the object that appears to your consciousness, your conceptual cognition of it may make you feel happy, but your idea itself did not produce this effect. This, then, is what it means for a metaphysical entity to be permanent.

Other examples of metaphysical entities are the empty space or place that something occupies and the Identitylessness of the conventional "I". Although such things can be thought about conceptually, an empty space or the Identitylessness of someone's conventional "I" can never appear directly as the object of your bare perception. Nevertheless they can be indirectly apprehended by such perception when there directly appears to one of your types of consciousness what occupies this space or the impermanence of the five aggregates that are known in terms of the conventional "I" that is void of this permanent identity. In this instance your bare perception directly apprehends the object that appears to it, an objective entity. The metaphysical entity that it apprehends indirectly is also considered its involved object, but it is not the appearing object of this bare perception. If a metaphysical entity actually appears clearly to your consciousness, then it is through a conceptual cognition that you know it.

Furthermore, bare perception is defined as an awareness that is non-deceptive and devoid of any conceptualizing. When divided there are four types (of bare perception): sensory, mental, that of awareness of consciousness and bare yogic perception.

As these four are non-deceptive, it is important first to know the causes for deception of which they are free.

The four causes for (a cognition to be) deceptive are its (1) reliance, (2) object, (3) situation and (4) immediate condition.

(1) A cognition may be deceptive through reliance on a defective organ. If you are cross-eyed you will see two moons. (2) If the object of your cognition is moving very quickly, such as a torch being whirled around in the dark, you may be deceived into seeing a ring of fire. (3) If you look out from a moving train, you may see trees approaching and rapidly receding. (4) If immediately before looking at something your mind is violently disturbed by anger you may see red or, with paranoia, threatening figures when no one is there. Bare perceptions are not affected by any such causes for deception.

The bare perception that arises (only) from one of the physical cognitive-sensors as its (exclusive) dominant condition is bare sensory perception. There are five types, from that which takes a visible form (as its object) to that which takes a bodily sensation.

Thus there are bare sensory perceptions of sights, sounds, smells, tastes and bodily sensations or touch.

Each of these as well has (divisions of) valid, subsequent and inattentive cognitions.

> When you see a vase non-deceptively and without conceptualizing about it, the first moment is your valid bare perception of it. From the second instant you have subsequent visual perception, while the last moment is inattentive. Seeing this vase while listening intently to music is also an example of an inattentive visual perception.

The bare perception that arises (only) from a mental sensor as its (exclusive) dominant condition is bare mental perception. There are five kinds such as the bare mental perception that takes a visible form (as its object) and so forth.

> When you remember, imagine or dream about a sight, sound, smell, taste or touch, the object of your cognition is an idea or mental image of these sense objects. In these cases you know a metaphysical entity by a conceptual cognition. However, with bare perception you are aware of an objective entity, one of these five actual types of sense objects, through the cognitive sensor of your mind without any conceptual cognition of it. You have such bare mental perception of a vase, for instance, immediately after your visual perception of it and just prior to conceptualizing about it. The stream of its continuity lasts only a very short time.

The bare perception of awareness of consciousness is (that which takes as its object only) the aspect of (conscious) takers (of objects), and which is non-deceptive and devoid of any conceptualizing. Both of these as well are explained as having three varieties each, namely valid cognition and so forth.

Bare yogic perception is the bare perception in the mindstream of an Ārya that arises from the power of meditating single-mindedly with joint mental quiescence and penetrative insight as its dominant condition.

> As explained previously, bare yogic perception has only initial valid and subsequent moments. It never is inattentive. It occurs only during the meditation session of an Ārya when he is completely focused on either subtle impermanence or on the coarse or subtle Identitylessness of his conventional "I".

When divided from the point of view of its basis, there are three (types, namely that) of Śrāvaka, Pratyekabuddha and Mahāyāna Āryas.

Both Śrāvakas and Pratyekabuddhas work for their own personal liberation from rebirth with suffering in cyclic existence. The former rely on a teacher throughout their entire training, while the latter during the final stages do not. Bodhisattvas, on the other hand, work to achieve the Full Enlightenment of Buddhahood in order to be able to liberate all others. According to the Sautrāntika explanation, when any one of these three achieves bare yogic perception of the Identitylessness of his conventional "I", he becomes an Ārya either of the Śrāvaka, Pratyekabuddha or Bodhisattva, that is the Mahāyāna, class according to his motivation and style of practice.

From the point of view of their natures, each of them also has three (sub-divisions: bare yogic perception) on the paths of seeing, meditation and no more learning.

Śrāvakas, Pratyekabuddhas and Bodhisattvas each progress to their goals through a five-fold path. When they have developed as their motivation a pure renunciation of the suffering of cyclic existence and its causes, Śrāvakas and Pratyekabuddhas enter their first path. According to the Mahāyāna tenets, Bodhisattvas enter theirs when in addition they develop a pure motivation of Bodhicitta, that is an enlightened motive of working to become a Buddha for the sake of all sentient beings. Although their motivations and goals are different, and thus from this point of view their paths are also different, nevertheless according to the Sautrāntikas each of these three follow similar practices on each of their five paths and develop the same wisdom.

On the first path, then, the path of accumulation, they develop single-minded concentration in mental quiescence meditation. On the second, the path of preparation, they gain conceptual cognition of the Identitylessness of their conventional "I", that is valid inferential understanding of this, in penetrative insight meditation. On the third, the path of seeing, they gain a bare yogic perception of this Identitylessness in their meditation state and become Āryas of their respective classes.

On the fourth path, that of meditation, they follow the Eightfold Path of the Āryas to overcome the obstacles preventing either their liberation or omniscience. They achieve these goals on the last path, that of perfection, when Śrāvakas and Pratyekabuddha Āryas overcome the former and become Arhats of each of these classes and Bodhisattva Āryas surmount both obstacles and become Buddhas. As Omniscient Buddhas they perceive the Identitylessness of their conventional "I" at all times.

From the point of view of their objects, there are two (types of bare yogic perception): that which knows which things exist and what they are like.

With bare yogic perception you can apprehend things either directly or indirectly. Directly, you can apprehend the object that appears to it. This is an objective entity, what a thing is, which by definition is an ultimate truth. What it apprehends indirectly does not actually appear to it. It is a metaphysical entity, what a thing is like, and as such is a conventional truth. Thus with bare yogic perception you directly apprehend the ultimate truth of the impermanence of your five aggregate physical and mental faculties which are known in terms of a conventional "I" lacking a permanent or substantially existing identity. Indirectly, you apprehend the conventional truth of this permanent Identitylessness of your conventional "I". Thus directly you apprehend what you are and indirectly how you exist.

8

Seemingly Bare Perception

The opposite (of bare perception) is seemingly bare perception. This is mutually inclusive with deceptive cognition and is defined as an awareness that is deceived with respect to its appearing object. It takes the appearance of something to be the actual thing itself. Distorted cognition, on the other hand, is deceived with respect to what actually exists, not merely with its appearance.

Both deceptive and distorted cognitions may be conceptual or non-conceptual. In a conceptual cognition the appearing object is a metaphysical entity, namely a mental image or idea, such as that of a vase. Its conceptualized-about object is the vase itself, an objective entity. Conceptual cognitions are deceptive in as much as they confuse an appearance with the actuality it implies, such as the mental image of a vase with an actual vase. If what a cognition conceptualizes about is non-existent, then it is not only deceptive, but distorted as well. An example is one in which the mental picture of a rabbit's horn is confused with an actual rabbit's horn, although there is no such thing.

Although all conceptual cognitions are deceptive, not all are distorted. In fact, some of them, such as inferential understandings, are valid cognitions in as much as they are an initial non-fraudulent awareness of their conceptualized-about object. Thus because such a cognition correctly and freshly apprehends its object, the vase, it is valid and in this respect not fraudulent. But because it confuses it with the mental image of a vase, it is deceptive.

In a non-conceptual valid bare perception directly apprehending a vase, for instance, the appearing and involved objects are the vase itself, an objective entity. Here it is not the conceptualized-about object. However, when a near-sighted person looks at this vase, he sees a

blurred object and thus has only non-conceptual seemingly bare perception. Relying on a defective sense organ, his perception is deceived because it confuses what
appears to it, a blurred vase, with what is actually there,
a vase. It is distorted as well because there is no such
thing as an actual blurred vase. It is non-conceptual because it does not mix the blurred vase that appears to it
with a mental image of one.

   There are seven types of seemingly bare perception,
six conceptual and one non-conceptual.

It says (in Dignāga's *Compendium of Validities [Pramāṇa-samuccaya]*):
"They are termed those that cognize (1) deceptions and (2) what is
screened, (3) those of inferential understandings and (4) derived
from inference, (5) those that are mindful of something (once more)
and (6) those that fancy ahead. There is also (7) the seemingly bare
perception that is blurred." The first six are conceptual seemingly
bare perceptions while the last, a knowing of something blurred, is
non-conceptual seemingly bare perception. For the meaning to be
understood (by each), you should refer to such (texts) as *A Filigree
of (Valid) Lines of Reasoning* (by His Holiness the First Dalai Lama).

   (1) Conceptual cognition of what is deceptive is distorted
   as well. It is the conceptual seemingly bare perception of
   anything that does not accord with fact, such as the misconception that sound is permanent. Also included in this
   category are ordinary people's dreams and fantasies
   which confuse fiction with reality.

      (2) Conceptual cognition of conventional things is not
   distorted. It is a correct apprehension of something conventional that is made of atoms or a collection of moments, such as a vase or a mental state. It is deceptive in
   that it mixes such an objective entity with a metaphysical idea of it.

      (3) All inferential understandings are conceptual cog-
   nitions in which you know something obscure and not
   readily obvious by relying on a valid line of reasoning.
   They are deceptive because they confuse their appearing object with their conceptualized-about object. For instance, you can validly know that sound is impermanent
   by relying on the reason: because it is a product of causes.
   You correctly reach this conclusion because the three fac-

tors of agreement, congruence and incongruence are satisfied. Being a product of causes is a property of sound, an exclusive characteristic of impermanent phenomena and never a quality of anything permanent. Your conceptual inference, then, has a mental image of these three factors as its appearing object. Although it is valid, it is deceptive because it mixes this with its conceptualized-about object, the actual logical pervasions that are the three validating factors.

A Buddha would not need to rely on such a conceptual cognition of an inferential understanding to know the impermanence of sound. When having a bare audial perception directly apprehending a sound, he would also directly apprehend its impermanence without any use of logic.

Another example of this third type of conceptual cognition is knowing an effect and saying that you know its cause, such as feeling the warmth of the rays of the sun and knowing by inference that the sun is hot. Also included is giving the name of an effect to its cause, such as calling a Buddha a Compassionate One. In this case you are mixing the effect of being a Buddha, that one is compassionate, with its cause, that one is a Buddha. Another example is thinking of sound as being the product of causes, which also mixes an effect with its cause.

(4) Conceptual cognitions derived from inferential understandings are your cognitions of the conclusions derived from the above process of inference. An example is your conceptual knowledge that sound is impermanent, gained after inferring this from the three validating factors.

(5) A conceptual cognition of being mindful of something once more mixes a mental image with the original event or object.

(6) One of fancying ahead about something in the future, or about what might have been if things were different, confuses a plan or an idea with the actuality of the present moment. Thus all six of these types of conceptual cognition are deceptive since they mix their appearing object with what they conceptualize about.

(7) A non-conceptual seemingly bare perception of a blurred object is also deceptive because what appears to it in actuality is not so.

Non-conceptual seemingly bare perception, a way of knowing in which something non-existent appears clearly, and non-conceptual distorted cognition are all mutually inclusive.

Furthermore, a conceptual cognition is a conceptual awareness that takes (its object) and mixes it with either a flimsy idea based on mere sounds or a firm idea based on understanding.

If you wish to specify something precisely so that it will not be confused with anything else, you would say that it is·what is left over after you have excluded or eliminated everything it is not. A mango is not an orange, a peach, an apricot, a canteloupe and so forth. These are all non-mangoes. When you exclude all the things that a mango is not, then what you are left with is the opposite of a non-mango, namely a mango itself. This is called the double negative of a mango and every permanent and impermanent phenomenon can be individually specified by its own double negative.

An idea of a mango is the mental picture or image you have of one based on the exclusion of everything it is not and which you use for conceptually thinking about one. It is not derived, however, from an active process of excluding but is merely a metaphysical entity. You can have a mental picture of a specific mango or of mangoes in general, and it can be of its shape, smell, taste and so forth. If you have actually seen or eaten one, then your idea of a mango is a firm one based on first-hand experience and understanding. If you have not, then you may have only a flimsy idea based on the sound of the word "mango" itself.

Double negatives, mental images and all sorts of ideas are metaphysical entities. They are permanent phenomena incapable of producing any effect. Thinking about your mental picture of a mango may make you hungry, but your idea of the fruit cannot fill your stomach. When you have bare visual perception of a mango, you see merely the mango itself, an objective entity. When you have conceptual cognition of it with your mind, you mix this objective entity with your idea of it. This is why it is deceptive, because the appearing object of such a cognition—an idea which appears clearly—and its conceptualized-about object—the mango itself which also appears, but only unclearly—are mixed together or superimposed one on the other.

Buddhas do not have conceptual cognition. Ideas or mental images do not exist in their mindstream, although they are able to perceive such metaphysical entities cognized by others. When they were sentient beings an idea of a mango may have become existent in their mindstream occasioned by their first hearing about or eating one. While this idea was present it was permanent in the sense that it could not produce any effect. When they became enlightened it disappeared and became totally non-existent. Buddhas, then, know everything through bare perception, either directly or indirectly.

When divided, there is the two-fold (classification) of conceptual cognitions that accord with fact and those that do not.

Conceptually thinking about a vase in terms of an idea of one is undistorted and conforms with fact or reality. This is true also of your conceptual cognition of Identitylessness arising from inference. Your mental image of the Identitylessness of your conventional "I" corresponds to its actual Identitylessness. But your conceptual cognition of a rabbit's horn, a permanent sound or the permanent identity of your conventional "I", on the other hand, is distorted in that it does not accord with fact.

(There is also) the two-fold (classification) of conceptual cognitions that apply names and those that apply facts.

(1) In a conceptual cognition that applies a name, you know the definition of something and take it for that which is being defined. An example is thinking this object with a fat belly, an indented flat base and from which I can pour water is a vase or a pitcher. (2) In one that applies a fact you know a quality or characteristic of something and take it for that which has this quality, such as thinking this blue porcelain object is a vase or that thing over there holding a stick is a man.

The conceptual cognition that mixes an actual vase with the idea of something having a fat belly, an indented flat base and from which water can be poured is one that applies both a name and a fact. This is because having a fat belly and so forth is both the definition and a qualitative description of a vase or a pitcher. But not all such cognitions applying a fact necessarily apply a name as well. An idea of a blue porcelain object can be applied when thinking conceptually about a vase, a bathtub or many such things and is not the definition of any of them.

There is also the three-fold (division) of conceptual cognitions involving a label and a basis, those that interpolate extraneous facts and conceptual cognitions involving obscure facts. There are many such classification schemes.

(1) In conceptual cognitions that involve a label and a basis you know something through its mental label. For instance, you know that four-legged animal with a great hump of flesh on its neck by the label "brahmin bull" or your five aggregates by the label of your conventional "I". Thus when your stomach is empty you think "I am hungry", mixing your idea of an "I" with your aggregates of form, feeling and so forth.

(2) The Tibetan word for interpolation literally means tying a feather to a bamboo arrow. Thus in an interpolated conceptual cognition you tie or superimpose an idea of some extra descriptive quality onto an object that is not qualified by it. For instance you may think of sound as something permanent or your conventional "I" as having a permanent identity. As these qualities do not apply to what you are ascribing them, such thoughts are conceptual distorted cognitions as well.

The opposite of interpolation is repudiation. With it you deny qualities of an object that pertain to it. Thus instead of thinking of sound as permanent, you would deny that it is impermanent. Interpolation and repudiation prevent you from cognizing a middle path of the actuality of things.

(3) In a conceptual cognition involving an obscure fact, you mix an object with one of its obscure attributes that you have not apprehended directly through bare

perception. For instance, if there is a man hiding behind a house and you have not seen him, but someone tells you he is there, you come to know something that is not obvious when you look at the house. Likewise when you gain a conceptual understanding from inference that sound is impermanent or that your conventional "I" lacks a permanent and substantially existing identity, you also know something that is not directly obvious to your bare perception. In such a conceptual cognition you mix an idea of an obscure quality, such as impermanence, with an object qualified by it, such as sound.

In addition, there is the three-fold (classification) of conceptual cognitions of what has been heard, contemplated about and meditated upon. The meaning of each in turn is (1) that which takes (its object) by means of a flimsy idea based on merely sound alone; (2) that which has found certainty (about it) from having contemplated its meaning; and (3) a higher state conceptual awareness (of an object attained) from having become more and more familiar with its meaning which has arisen from contemplation.

Your Guru tells you about the Identitylessness of your conventional "I". Based merely on the teachings you have heard, you now have a flimsy idea of what this means based on the mere sound of his words. When conceptually you are aware of Identitylessness in terms of such an idea alone, then you have the conceptual cognition of it that arises from hearing. This is also an example of presuming something true to be so for a correct reason, but without knowing why.

When you have contemplated the meaning of what you have heard through the use of valid logical arguments such as inference, you will gain a confident conceptual or intellectual understanding of what Identitylessness means. You will then have the conceptual cognition of it that arises from contemplation. This will be through the medium of a firm idea based on understanding.

Through repeated inference you will gain a thorough familiarity with the meaning of Identitylessness. When you have achieved a state of mental quiescence and the higher attainments of meditative concentration, you can then focus your single-minded concentration on your fully confident and familiar conceptual understanding. This will then be the conceptual cognition of Identitylessness that arises from meditation.

If in addition to the collection of insight you have accumulated from such meditational practice as this, you have also built up a vast collection of merit from having done many virtuous deeds with pure motivation over a long period of time, you will then as a result achieve bare yogic perception. This comes about not mystically through a leap of faith, but simply through a process of cause and effect. Your single-minded concentration on your conceptual understanding that the conventional "I" by which your five aggregates are validly known lacks a permanent substantially existing identity will then automatically become a bare yogic perception. Thus single-mindedly and non-conceptually you will directly apprehend the impermanence of your aggregates void of a conventional "I" having such an identity and indirectly its Identitylessness. With this achievement you become an Ārya, a Noble One.

9

The Number of Valid Ways of Knowing

The types of distorted conceptual cognitions that have arisen concerning how many (distinct ways constitute) the count of valid ways of knowing are as follows. The Cārvākas and Jains accept only one valid way of knowing, namely bare perception.

> In not accepting inferential understanding as valid, the Cārvākas and Jains assert that you can only know things that are obvious. If you cannot directly see something or hear it and so forth, they say you cannot know it.

The Sāṃkhyas assert that there are three valid ways: (1) bare perception, (2) inferential understanding and (3) knowing something through verbal indication.

> When you understand what someone means by what he says or you learn something that is true by reading it in a text of scriptural authority or hearing it explained by someone trustworthy, you have known something by a verbal indication. The Sautrāntikas classify such knowledge under inferential understanding, but the Sāṃkhyas and many other non-Buddhist schools classify this as a separate valid means of knowing.
>
> Included in this category is not only the knowledge of what someone means when you hear him speaking in the next room, for instance, but also knowing that he is there. However, according to the Buddhist explanation of the Sautrāntikas, you can apprehend such knowledge indirectly when you have bare audial perception of his voice.

The Nyāyas (and Vaiśeṣikas) accept four, adding to these three (4) understanding something through analogy.

> You have never seen a zebra. You go to a zoo and see an animal that looks like a mule but has black and white stripes. You know what a mule is and by its analogy you know that this strange animal is not a mule. This is to

know something by analogy. You do not exactly know what your object is, but by analogy with other objects you do know, you can identify what it is not.

(Some of) the Mīmāṁsakas claim that the number is definitely only six: these four plus (5) validly understanding something by implication and (6) validly knowing an absence.

(5) The fat man Devadatta does not eat during the day. Because Devadatta is fat and because people must eat in order to be fat and can do so during either the day or the night, you know by implication or disjunctive reasoning that Devadatta must eat at night. Another example is you know someone is in your two-room house, but you do not see him in the front room. By implication or a process of elimination you know he must be in the back one.

(6) There are four types of absences: prior, disintegrated, mutually exclusive and absolute. The Mīmāṁsakas say that there is a separate means of cognition for validly knowing such absences. For instance, when you see milk you can know of the prior absence of yoghurt in it, that is the yoghurt's not yet being in the milk before it has curdled. Later when you see the yoghurt you know of the disintegrated absence of the milk in it, for once it has curdled the milk is no longer there. When you know of the mutually exclusive absence of a horse in a bull, you see that a bull is not a horse and a horse could not be a bull for these two are mutually exclusive. When you see a rabbit's head and know of the absolute absence of a rabbit's horn on it, you know of the absence of something that does not exist. Although you might fantasize and see a mental image of a goat's horn on a rabbit's head, you cannot possibly imagine a rabbit's horn there, because there is no such thing.

The Cāraka (Mīmāṁsakas) claim that the number is definitely eleven. To the above six they add validly knowing something by (7) common sense, (8) non-perception, (9) tradition, (10) inclusion and (11) intuition.

(7) With valid inferential understanding you use analytic reasoning to infer the cause from an effect, for instance where there is smoke there must be fire. The reverse of

this is to know something by synthetic reasoning or common sense, which is to deduce the effect from a cause. An example is where there is fire there must be smoke. With the former, then, you reason backwards from an effect to its cause; with the latter you reason forwards from a cause to its effect or just know this through common sense.

(8) If you do not perceive something when if it were there you would, then you know by non-perceptioñ that it is not there. For instance, you can know of the absence of horns on a rabbit's head by your non-perception of them, because if they were there you would surely see them. This is different from simply knowing the absolute absence of a rabbit's horns, where you know something because of the absence of an object. Here you know something because of the absence of a valid means of cognizing it.

(9) When you know something by tradition, you believe something to be true because everyone else does. An example is knowing that a certain tree contains a spirit because all your ancestors and everyone in your community believe it does. Also you know by tradition to shake hands with your right hand, and to feed a cold and starve a fever.

(10) When you know something by inclusion, you know about the individuals included in a group by knowing about the group itself. An example is knowing that there are at least ten people in the classroom when you are sure there are fifty, or that a certain person is Japanese because you know he is a member of a Japanese delegation to a conference.

(11) If for no apparent reason you have a feeling that your mother will visit you today and she actually does, then you knew she was coming by intuition. Although such cognitions do occur, they are unreliable and usually a form of wishful thinking. It is by coincidence that they are true, because more often than not, unless you have achieved the higher attainments of meditative concentration, your expectations or predictions are false.

Our own tradition is that it is definite that there are only two: bare perception and inferential understanding.

The reason there are only these two is because there are only two kinds of validly knowable or validly cognizable things—objective and metaphysical entities. The former are objects that are obvious and can be apprehended directly through bare perception. The latter may be either objective or metaphysical, but are either obscure, such as the impermanence of sound, or extremely obscure, such as the fact that wealth is the result of generosity practised during previous lives. Such things cannot be apprehended directly through bare perception, although by Āryas they may be indirectly so perceived. Ordinary people know them through inference and thus it is necessary for there to be only two distinct valid ways of knowing. To differentiate more as separate methods is superfluous.

Concerning this, the definition of a valid way of knowing is a fresh non-fraudulent awareness. When divided, there are two types: valid bare perception and inferential understanding. From another point of view, there are (another) two types: validly knowing that the attentiveness (of a cognition) either has been self-induced or will have to be induced by another (cognition). And from the point of view of etymology, there are three types: valid people, speech and cognitions.

You may know something validly by relying on either valid persons, speech or cognition. A valid person is a Buddha. Valid speech is his teachings, such as those in the first turning of the wheel of Dharma concerning the Four Noble Truths. The four are the truths of suffering, its cause, its cessation and the path leading to this. Reliance on such persons or speech will lead you to valid knowledge. You will attain this as well through the valid cognitions of bare perception and inferential understanding.

These three types of knowledge are valid in the sense that they arise from valid sources. But since your cognition of what Buddha has said may be presumptive or inattentive, these are said to be valid only in an etymological sense and not in an actual one.

10

Inferential Understanding

Inferential understanding is the comprehension of an obscure fact through reliance on a correct line of reasoning as its basis. When divided, three types are explained: inferential understandings based on (1) the force of evidence, (2) renown and (3) conviction.

(1) To know directly something obscure and not readily obvious, you must rely on the valid support of either logical evidence, renown or conviction. For instance, when your neighbor is making a great deal of noise you may become annoyed and impatient because it is not obvious that sound is impermanent. However, if you rely on the force of evidence you can prove to yourself that this noise will pass simply because it is man-made. To do so you must rely on the three factors of agreement, congruence and incongruence. This noise was made by a man; everything man-made must pass; and nothing man-made has endured forever. Therefore through this first type of inferential understanding you can be certain that this noise will also pass. With such valid knowledge you can then control your anger.

(2) Just as Westerners have traditionally seen a "man in the moon" when looking at its craters, Indians have seen a "rabbit in the moon". When in Sanskrit and Tibetan literature you read about "that which has a rabbit", these words do not refer to their obvious, literal meaning. You know that such a literary allusion refers to the moon through an inferential understanding based on renown or a popular convention. In Western literature you know that a man's best friend is his dog through a similar valid means. This is also the method by which you know what any word means when you hear it, for all words are popular conventions.

(3) There are certain things that are extremely obscure and only when you become a Buddha can you have bare perception of them. Before that you must rely on

your conviction in the Buddhas' scriptural texts to know them at all. Since Buddhas are valid persons and what they have said is valid speech, you can infer that by relying on them you will have valid cognition. Thus through an inferential understanding based on conviction, you can be sure that prosperity is the result of previously practised generosity.

(1) Inferential understanding and (2) valid inferential understanding are to be known as mutually inclusive.

Therefore all inferential understandings relying on correct lines of reasoning are valid.

11

Self and Other Induced Attentiveness

Valid ways of knowing self- and other-attentiveness are the valid knowing that the attentiveness has either been self-induced or will have to be induced by the power of another (cognition concerning the fact) that if the significance (or what an object is) were not established on that object it cognizes, (the cognition of this object as having that significance) could not arise.

These two valid ways of knowing amount to knowing that it either is or is not self-evident what something is. For instance, there is a fire in the distance. When you look at it, you can either be attentive of it as simply being a red object or as being a fire. When you see it in the former way, but not in the latter, you can validly know two things about this object. You can be aware that the attentiveness of it as being red has been self-induced, which means to realize that it is self-evident that the object is red. You validly know that if its significance as red were not established on it, you could not have seen it as red. Furthermore, if from where you are standing you cannot be sure whether this object is a fire or a red cloth, you can also be validly aware of the fact that the attentiveness of it as a fire will have to be induced by the power of another cognition. In other words, you realize that only by having a closer look can you become attentive of the fact that if it were not a fire you could not see it as a fire. Thus when seeing this item as merely a red object you can validly know that it is not self-evident that it is a fire.

Another example is seeing a tree at a distance. That it is a tree is self-evident and you validly know that your attentiveness of it as such has been self-induced. But it is not self-evident that it is an oak and you are aware that the attentiveness of it as an oak or an elm will have to be induced by another cognition. Only when you come closer will you know for sure.

A valid way of knowing that attentiveness has been self-induced must be one of five types of valid cognition. Either it is a valid bare perception of (1) awareness of consciousness or (2) yogic, or it is (3) an inferential understanding or (a valid bare sensory perception) of (4) something with its functioning (also) appearing or (5) something with which you are familiar.

(1) When your faculty of awareness of consciousness has fresh bare perception of a state of consciousness, its attentiveness is self-induced. No further cognition is necessary.

(2) The same is true of valid bare yogic perception cognizing either subtle impermanence or the coarse or subtle Identitylessness of your person or conventional "I". If the attentiveness of what was apprehended by such perception were not self-induced, you could not have apprehended it at all.

(3) With valid inferential understanding you reach a correct conclusion from a valid line of reasoning. Nothing further is required to know this conclusion, therefore your attentiveness of it is self-induced.

(4) When you have bare sensory perception of the manifestation of something's ability to produce an effect, such as a fire's consumption of fuel, you are directly perceiving what is happening. If it required another cognition to know what it was you were perceiving, then you could not say you were actually witnessing the manifestation of such an effect. You would not know specifically what you were perceiving at all.

(5) If you have seen your friend's son every day and are totally familiar with him, then whenever you have valid bare sensory perception of him, even at a distance, it is self-evident that he is the son of your friend. If you are a master repairman, then whenever you see a broken appliance you know immediately what is wrong and how to repair it. Because of your complete familiarity, your attentiveness of the problem is self-induced without the need of further cognition.

When divided from the point of view of etymology, there are three kinds of valid ways of knowing that attentiveness will have to be induced by another (cognition). These are bare perception of something (1) for the first time, (2) when your mind is unheedful and (3) having a cause for deception.

(1) When you see an utpala lotus for the first time, it is self-evident that it is a blue flower, but not what specific kind it is. To realize when you see this that you will need further information and cognition to identify it is an example of this first type of knowing that the attentiveness of its species will have to be other-induced.

(2) The second type occurs, for instance, when someone says something to you while you are engrossed in thinking about something else. Aware that you have heard something, you realize that it will have to be repeated for you to become attentive of what has been said. Such valid cognition often occurs with inattentive perception.

(3) When you see a mirage of water in a desert and realize that you will need to have a closer look to be certain of what you have seen, this is an example of knowing that your attentiveness will have to be other-induced when your perception is affected by a cause for deception.

These last two types of cognition are valid in the sense that with them you realize that what you are perceiving is not self-evident. But because the cognitions themselves are inattentive or distorted, they are valid only in an etymological sense and not in an actual one.

There are also the valid ways of knowing that the attentiveness of (1) what if the appearance of something is self-induced, but what it is in truth will have to be other-induced; (2) what something is in general is self-induced, but what it is specifically will have to be other-induced; and (3) whether something has even appeared will have to be other-induced. Although such (ways of knowing) have been explained, care is needed in differentiating which are actually (valid) and which are (only) nominally so.

(1) An example of this first type is seeing something red in the distance. What appears to your bare sensory perception, a red color, is self-evidently red, but that this is in fact a fire is not self-evident. Thus when seeing this object you can validly know both that your attentiveness

of how it appears has been self-induced, but what it is in truth will have to be other-induced.

(2) The second is seeing a tree in the distance. What it is in general, a tree, is self-evident. To know specifically that it is an oak, you will have to go closer.

(3) You see a man on a hill out of the corner of your eye. Unsure if you actually have seen a man, you realize you will have to look at the hill more carefully to be certain. This is an example of the third type. Another one is seeing someone and, wondering if you have ever seen him before, realizing that you will need to have another look to be sure.

These first two are actual valid ways of knowing something. But to realize that the attentiveness of whether something has even appeared to you will have to be induced by another cognition is only nominally called valid. In actuality it is inattentive or may even be distorted.

Although it is pervasive that the valid knowing of other-induced attentiveness is a valid way of knowing, yet because that valid knowing of other-induced attentiveness with respect to (the cognition of) some phenomenon may not (involve) a valid way of knowing that (object), precise detail is required concerning the pervasions and so forth.

Thus you may invalidly know something, such as a mirage, but validly realize you will have to look at it again to be certain what it is. This is valid from the point of view of correctly knowing that the attentiveness will have to be induced by another cognition. But because it is based on a distorted cognition, this cannot actually be considered valid.

12

Objects of Cognition

There are four types of objects that can be known: (1) appearing, (2) assumed-aspect, (3) conceptualized-about and (4) involved objects. Appearing and assumed-aspect objects are mutually inclusive. Such appearances as that of falling hairs which do not rely on an external object (do not involve a concrete assumable item present), but aside from that they and all cognitions have an appearing object.

> In general, cognitions may be divided into sensory and mental. Each of these include valid and invalid cognitions, correct apprehensions and distortions. Sensory cognitions are never conceptual. They may be either valid bare perceptions or subsequent, inattentive or distorted ones. When they are distorted, they may or may not rely on a concrete item before them. For instance, seeing a white conch shell as yellow relies on the external object of a conch shell, the aspect of which is assumed with the incorrect color. But for a person with cataracts who has the false feeling of hair falling over his eyes, the appearing and assumed-aspect object is falling hair, although there is no concrete assumable falling hair present before him as the basis for his distorted cognition.
>
> Thus every type of sensory, as well as every mental cognition has an appearing object the aspect of which it is assuming. The appearing object of a non-distorted sensory cognition and of a non-conceptual mental one is an objective entity such as a vase. The appearing object of a conceptual mental cognition is a metaphysical entity, such as a mental image or an idea of a vase. These, then, are the aspects that the consciousness of these cognitions assume and thus appearing objects are synonymous with assumed-aspect ones.

Conceptualized-about objects are phenomena (that arise exclu sively) through the gateway of conceptual cognition. They exist i all conceptual cognitions that accord with fact.

The appearing object of a conceptual cognition, then, is a mental image such as idea of a vase. The conceptualized-about object is what this is a mental picture of, in this case an actual objective vase. Conceptual cognitions that do not conform to reality, such as one of a rabbit's horn, are distorted. Although an image of such a horn is the appearing object of such mental consciousness, the conceptualized-about object, the actual rabbit horn, does not in fact exist.

Involved objects (knowable) by valid cognitions are clear-cut factual items. All valid ways of knowing and all persons with (such valid knowledge) have this (type of object).

Every cognition has not only an appearing object, the aspect of which it assumes, but also an involved object. To the valid bare perception of a vase, the appearing object is an actual objective vase, which appears clearly. This is directly apprehended and is the involved object. If this cognition also indirectly apprehends the metaphysical entity of the absence of flowers in the vase, this absence will also be the involved object of that cognition. But it will not be the appearing or assumed-aspect objects because metaphysical entities cannot appear to bare perception. Both the vase and the absence of flowers in it are clear-cut factual items because they can be involved objects of a valid way of knowing.

The subsequent bare perception of a vase and the absence of flowers in it has both of these clear-cut factual items as its involved objects since it is a cognition with apprehension. The former will appear and the latter will not. But during the inattentive visual perception of the vase, the only involved object is the vase itself. It still appears clearly but is not paid attention. Since this mind is not an apprehension it cannot be involved with the metaphysical absence. There are no conceptualized-about objects in either the valid, subsequent or inattentive bare perceptions of the vase, because these ways of knowing are all non-conceptual.

In the non-conceptual distorted visual perception of a blue snow mountain, the snow mountain itself is the appearing object and aspect assumed. Also appearing clearly is this object as being blue, whereas in fact it is white. Thus the appearance as a whole, the blue snow-mountain, is the involved object of this distortion and it is non-existent. There is no conceptualized-about object because this mind is non-conceptual.

When you see an object and conclude it is a vase because it has a fat belly, a flat indented base and can be used to pour water, the first instance of such knowledge is a valid inferential understanding based on popular convention and also a conceptual cognition based on semantics. The appearing object of this cognition is the metaphysical entity of a mental image of the vase, and this is the aspect it assumes. Through the medium of this image, it knows its involved object, the vase itself, which appears only unclearly to this cognition because it is deceptively mixed with the mental image. The vase thus is the conceptualized-about object. The analysis of the objects remains the same for the subsequent cognition of this conceptual inferential understanding.

In the distorted conceptual cognition of a blue snow mountain, the appearing and assumed-aspect objects are a mental image of a blue snow mountain, which appears clearly. The involved and conceptualized-about objects are an actual snow mountain which does not exist at all and does not even appear unclearly as in the case of the conceptual cognition of the vase.

Thus although the conceptualized-about object of a (non-distorted) conceptual cognition appears (unclearly) to that conceptual cognition, it is not its appearing object. Likewise, although its appearing object is what is conceptualized, it is not its conceptualized-about object.

In the non-distorted conceptual cognition of a vase, then, the conceptualized-about object is the vase itself, which appears only unclearly. What appears clearly is a mental image of the vase, which is both the appearing object and what is conceptualized. These distinctions should be noted.

13

The Conditions for Cognition to Arise

Bare sensory perceptions have three conditions (for their arisal): the objective, dominant and immediate conditions.

What causes you in general to have the cognitions you do is your previous karma. As the result of your past actions you experience things in the present. These three types of conditions are what help bring about the cognitions caused by your karma.

In the bare sensory perception taking a form (as its object), the condition of (something) displaying an aspect of itself is its objective condition. An example of what is being defined would be, for instance, something such as a form.

Thus the objective condition for the bare sensory perception of a vase is the vase itself. In the distorted sensory perception of a person with cataracts seeing hair falling over his eyes, there is no objective condition because there is no hair falling as an external object. Such distorted perception arises from other conditions independent of an objective one.

The condition that by its own power generates such a bare sensory perception is its dominant condition. It has two dominant conditions, a shared and an unshared one. The former would be the mental (sensor that serves) as its dominant condition and the latter, for instance, the eye-sensors.

In a general sense the cognitive sensor of the mind, as consciousness, can be the dominant or main condition for any bare mental or sensory perception taking any kind of object, a form, a sound and so forth. Thus it is shared or unspecialized. On the other hand, the physical cognitive sensors of the eyes are its unshared or specialized dominant condition since they serve as such. Any bare sensory perception, then, has two dominant conditions for its arising. A specific visual one, for instance, relies on the unshared dominant condition of the eye-sensors and the shared one of the non-physical cognitive sensor of the mind.

The condition that generates the clarity and awareness (factors) of such a bare sensory perception is the third (or immediate condition), for example the mental cognition that occurred immediately before it.

When you have sensory cognition of a vase, the first instance is your bare perception of it, an initial valid way of knowing. The next moments are subsequent cognitions and the last is inattentive. This sequence is followed immediately by a tiny moment of inattentive, non-conceptual mental cognition also taking this form. The immediate condition for the initial bare sensory perception is the conceptual mental cognition that immediately preceded it and with which you had the intention to look at the vase. The immediate condition for each of the subsequent moments is the cognition that came directly before it.

As for such things as bare sensory perceptions grasping sounds and so forth, (their conditions are to be understood) in a similar fashion.

From the Cittamātra point of view, the main and immediate conditions (or bare sensory perception) are explained in almost the same way (as that of the Sautrāntikas). However, these two systems differ in that they have separate ways of accepting whether there is an actual objective condition or only a nominal one.

Using skilful means Buddha taught many different systems of theories, each giving a progressively more refined level of explanation concerning the mind and other topics. In the Sautrāntika one, Buddha explained that there were substantially existing external objects and thus all bare sensory perceptions have an actual objective condition for their arisal. However, from the Cittamātra point of view Buddha explained that in the sense that nothing can exist independently of being cognized or cognizable, there actually are no external objects as such.

From the Sautrāntika point of view, cognitions arise from their potential which has been planted in your mindstream in the form of karmic instincts or seeds. According to the Cittamātra explanation, such instincts are planted specifically in your foundation consciousness (ālayavijñāna), which is another type of primary consciousness that each sentient being possesses. These instincts, however, are not only for the conscious portion of your cognitions—that is their primary consciousness, secondary mental factors and awareness of consciousness—but also for their objects. This is because, in a certain sense, objects of cognition cannot exist separately from your cognition of them. Therefore, according to this theory the objective of a cognition is only nominal because it does not exist as an external object. The object of a cognition, then, does not precede or cause your cognition of it, as the Sautrāntikas would explain, but rather the two occur simultaneously.

These explanations concerning external objects, foundation consciousness and the nominal existence of objective conditions are further refined in the Mādhyamika theories of the Svātantrikas and Prāsaṅgikas.

As for how the bare mental perception discussed here arises, there are (two traditions concerning) the bare mental perception (that comes) from the second phase of bare sensory perception onwards. (One is that) bare sensory and mental perception arise in alternation and (the other is) the way that Gyän (K'än-po) asserts bare mental perception, namely that three go together. Neither of these are accepted by our own tradition, which asserts instead that it arises only at the end of a stream of continuity of bare sensory perception.

According to the explanation tradition of alternating arisal, you first have a valid initial phase of bare visual perception of a vase, for instance. This is followed by alternating moments of subsequent visual and bare mental perceptions of the vase, one after the other. The Indian master Gyän K'än-po explained, however, that after an initial phase of valid bare visual perception you have three cognitions going together, namely simultaneous subsequent visual cognition, bare mental perception and the bare perception of awareness of consciousness.

The tradition followed here does not accept either position. Rather it asserts that, following this initial valid phase of bare visual perception, there is a second phase of subsequent visual cognition ending with a moment of inattentive bare perception. Only at the conclusion of such a sequence does the tiniest moment of bare mental perception arise, and for ordinary beings this is always inattentive.

The differences between conceptual and non-conceptual cognition can more or less be known from what has been said above. Both sensory cognition and bare perception may only be non-conceptual, whereas mental cognition is of two kinds, either conceptual or non-conceptual.

14

Secondary Mental Factors

There are primary consciousnesses and secondary mental factors.

In any cognition there are always these two kinds of conscious phenomena, which are concomitant, by means of sharing five things in common. They have a common (1) object, (2) reliance, (3) aspect, (4) time and (5) immediate source.

In a bare visual perception of a blue vase you have both primary visual consciousness and such secondary mental factors as recognition, feeling and so forth. (1) These all take the blue vase as their common object. They arise from the same objective condition. (2) They share a common dominant condition as well, for they all rely on the cognitive power of your eyes. (3) They take on the same aspect of the object that appears. (4) They occur at the same time, although to be more precise they are not exactly simultaneous. And (5) they arise from the same immediate source, namely the potential for this cognition in your mindstream.

When you place a clear piece of glass over a blue cloth, the glass takes on the same blue aspect as the cloth. If placed on a yellow cloth it would take on a yellow aspect, although the glass itself is neither blue nor yellow. A conscious phenomenon is like a clear piece of glass. Although it has no physical qualities of its own, it takes on whatever aspect of an object that appears to it. In any specific moment of cognition, then, both the primary consciousness and all its attendant secondary mental factors take on the same aspect of the object that appears.

Two things are said to have a single immediate source if they share a common, immediately preceding fundamental cause. The fundamental cause of a pot is the clay from which it is made. The light of two bulbs in a fixture are of one immediate source, since they both light up simultaneously when you switch on the electricity. Similarly, the primary consciousness and secondary mental factors of a cognition all "light up" simultaneously when their common potential is activated. According to the Cittamātra explanation, the object of the cognition as well shares this same immediate source.

Although the primary consciousness and secondary mental factors of a cognition share these five things in common, they are not identical, for their double negatives are different. The same is true with respect to the Cittamātra explanation of a conscious phenomenon and its object. Although consciousness and its object share a single immediate source, a seed of karmic instinct planted in your foundation consciousness, and in this respect are non-dual, this does not mean they are identical. This is because "subject" and "object" have different double negatives. Thus when you exclude everything that is not the subject and everything that is not the object, you are left with two different things.

Primary consciousness, the mind and consciousness are synonymous terms that are mutually inclusive. When divided, there are six types, from visual consciousness to mental consciousness.

With primary consciousness you are aware simply of the fundamental data of anything that can be validly cognized. The six types accepted by the Sautrāntikas are the visual, audial, olfactory, gustatory, tactile and mental. The enlightened motive of Bodhicitta is also a primary consciousness, having as its object the attainment of Buddhahood for the sake of all sentient beings. It is classified as a type of primary mental consciousness.

In some of the Cittamātra explanations, Buddha taught eight types of consciousness, adding foundation and delusion consciousness to these six. The former cognizes all objects roughly with inattentive perception and, as that in which seeds of karmic instinct are planted, is the foundation for and accompanies all cognitions. It was unspecified by Buddha to be either virtuous or non-virtuous since it is the source of both types of thoughts. The latter is what in delusion cognizes the former as being permanent and substantially existent from its own individual stance.

There are fifty-one secondary mental factors, namely the five ever-recurring, the five object-attentive, the eleven virtuous, the six root deluded, the twenty auxiliary deluded and the four changeable mental factors.

> With a secondary mental factor you are aware of distinctions and qualities in an object, the fundamental data of which you cognize with a primary consciousness. There are a great number of such factors which have been condensed into various lists. This particular enumeration of fifty-one derives from *A Compendium of General Knowledge* (*Abhidharmasamuccaya*) by Asanga. Among the many items not specifically mentioned here is karma, which is defined as the secondary mental factor bringing about virtuous and non-virtuous actions as well as the results of these actions. It is usually subsumed under the category of mental impulse.

Feeling, recognition, mental impulse, mental application and contact make five. Because these (always) come in the company of every (instance of) principal (or primary) consciousness, they are called the five ever-recurring secondary mental factors.

> Feeling is the experience of happiness, unhappiness or indifference in response to pleasurable, painful or neutral contact with an object of cognition. It is how you experience the ripening of your virtuous, non-virtuous or unspecified karma. Feelings may be either disturbing or undisturbing depending on whether you are attached to your contaminated aggregates or have gained bare yogic perception of Identitylessness.
>
> Recognition is what grasps the significance of an object that appears to either a conceptual or a non-conceptual cognition and identifies or labels it with either a conventional name or a meaning. Mental impulse is what moves the attention of your primary consciousness towards a potential object of cognition in accordance with your karmic instincts. Mental application makes the specific choice as to what you will cognize, accepting and rejecting alternatives, and determines how you will take your object. Contact is what connects to primary consciousness the secondary mental factors and awareness of consciousness, as well as objects of cognition and the

cognitive sensors. It may be either pleasurable, painful or neutral depending on your previous karma.

Every moment of cognition is accompanied by these five. Thus whenever you know something, a mental impulse has moved your attention towards it and mental application has made the specific choice as to how to cognize it. You have had pleasurable, painful or neutral contact with it and experienced this with a feeling of either happiness, unhappiness or indifference. And with recognition you have grasped the significance of what your have experienced. Moreover you are aware of all this through awareness of consciousness, which is what actually witnesses and experiences these feelings and so forth, allowing you afterwards to remember them.

Intention, fervent regard, mindfulness, fixation and the wisdom of discriminating awareness make five. It is explained that because these are attentive of your involvement with specific objects they are called five object-attentive secondary mental factors.

Intention is the wish to have a specific thing as the object of your cognition. Fervent regard is firmly cherishing such an object and wishing to preserve it. Mindfulness or memory keeps you from forgetting a specific object with which you are familiar. It refers to the conscious activity of remembering or being continually mindful of something, not the passive storage of impressions. Fixation is the placing of your attention on a specific object of cognition for any length of time. When perfected it becomes single-minded concentration. The wisdom of discriminating awareness analyses a particular object, discriminating between what is to be accepted or rejected and which actions are to be practised or avoided. When perfected it becomes the wisdom of understanding Identitylessness and Voidness, thus accepting the actual way in which all things exist and rejecting false distorted notions of true independent identities and existence. The wisdom of discriminating awareness is often referred to as common sense intelligence.

Respectful belief, a sense of propriety and self-respect, a sense of decency and consideration, the three roots of virtue—detachment,

imperturbability and open-mindedness—enthusiastic perseverance, flexibility of mind, care and awareness, clearminded tranquility and sympathy (are the eleven virtuous mental factors). Each
of these is virtuous from the point of view of being either an oppo-
nent (force against a non-virtuous state of mind) or by nature or
concomitant with (a virtuous one) and so forth.

Respectful belief is the positive attitude you have towards
objects that are virtuous and worthy of respect. Depending on whether it is motivated by no apparent reason, an
emotionally unstable state of mind or sound reasons well
understood, it is known as uncritical faith, longing faith
or conviction.

A sense of propriety and self-respect is your concern
for the consequences of your actions on yourself. A sense
of decency and consideration is your concern for such
consequences on others.

Detachment is the attitude of not clinging to objects
of cognition, being neither covetous nor possessive. With
imperturbability you never become angry with or hos-
tile towards any human being. With open-mindedness
you are never unwilling to learn. As the roots of all virtue they are the absence of the three poisons, namely
desire, hostility and closed-mindedness.

With enthusiastic perseverance you exert great effort in performing virtuous actions and take pleasure in
so doing. Flexibility of mind is the power to control and
use your mind in any virtuous manner you wish. When
perfected in mental quiescence meditation, it results in a
feeling of physical ecstasy and exhilarating mental bliss.

With care and awareness, conscientiousness, discre-
tion or prudence, you feel concern and take care about
your own virtues. Clearminded tranquility is a state of
mind temporarily free from mental dullness and mental
agitation. With sympathy you feel great concern for the
welfare of others.

Of these eleven, all are opponents to specific non-
virtuous states of mind. Thus respectful belief is the op-
ponent to disrespect, detachment to desire and so forth.
Flexibility of mind, care and awareness and clearminded
tranquility, however, become virtuous by means of being concomitant with or sharing five things in common

with other virtuous states of mind. For instance, care and awareness becomes virtuous by means of it being present with detachment, enthusiastic perseverance and so forth. Lastly, except for flexibility of mind and clearminded tranquility, the other nine are virtuous by nature. These two exceptions are not necessarily always virtuous, because they may also accompany non-virtuous or deluded mental states such as when feeling attachment for deep concentrations.

Desire, anger, pride, ignorance, deluded indecisive wavering and the speculative delusions are the six root deluded secondary mental factors. They are the main (attitudes) that bring your mindstream to a state of delusion.

Desire is regarding something impure and contaminated as being worthwhile and attractive. Anger is the generation of a violent or agitated attitude with respect to any object of cognition, animate or inanimate. When such anger is directed specifically towards another human being, this is called hostility. With pride you feel you are unique and special, better than everyone else.

Ignorance is the attitude of being unaware of Identitylessness and subtle change, the actual way in which all things exist. It is the root of continuing rebirth with suffering in cyclic existence. Included under this delusion is closed-mindedness, the foolish attitude of stubbornly closing yourself off from learning something new and potentially threatening.

With deluded indecisive wavering you fluctuate between two conclusions concerning the object of your cognition and are either inclined towards the incorrect conclusion or evenly balanced between the two. Thus in a state of nervous indecision concerning an object of virtue, you either head towards distortion and non-virtue or are left in a state of paralysis of the mind, unable to decide or do anything.

A delusion is defined as any secondary mental factor that when developed brings about suffering and uneasiness either to yourself or others. These first five root ones are known as the five non-speculative delusions.

Their distorted theoretical bases are the five speculative delusions.

The first is false views of transitory collections. It is to regard that which changes as being your concrete ego-identity. This is your mistaken view of who it is you think you are. Your five aggregate physical and mental faculties are constantly changing. However, with this speculative delusion you single out certain aspects of your aggregates and identify them with your conventional "I". Looking at yourself from the viewpoint of this "I", you regard what you identify with as being your concrete ego-identity. Thus you view everything as truly existing in terms of "me" and "mine".

The second speculative delusion is extreme views. Grasping at your supposedly concrete ego-identity, you either cling to it as something permanent or, closed-mindedly and defensively, deny it completely.

The third is views of false supremacy. It is to believe that the first two speculative delusions are supreme views and that indulgence of your ego-identity will lead to liberation from suffering. Grasping at that which changes as being your concrete ego-identity and feeling that this is the type of person you will always be, you believe that if you act according to this personality you will attain liberation. For instance, with the first speculative delusion you identify yourself as someone young and strong. With the second you feel that this is the way you will always be. With the third, then, you would feel that if you could always keep yourself physically fit and looking young and attractive, you will solve all your problems and never be unhappy.

The fourth speculative delusion is views of false morality and behavior as supreme. It is to hold the mistaken view that improper discipline and vowed conduct will lead to liberation from suffering. With such a delusion you would stand on one foot all day or sleep on a bed of nails and regard it as a true path to liberation.

The last is to hold distorted views. This is to believe that that which is always true and is always the case is never true and never the case. Such distorted views would be, for instance, to deny the law of cause and effect, to believe that there is no such thing as liberation from suffering and so forth.

These, then, are the root delusions, the main things that delude your mind and bring you suffering.

Hatred, resentment, concealment of non-virtues, outrage, jealousy, miserliness, concealment of shortcomings, pretentiousness, smugness, merciless cruelty, shamelessness, inconsideration, muddleheadedness, mental agitation, disrespect, laziness, recklessness, forgetfulness, inattentiveness, and mental wandering make twenty. As these are proximate to, develop from and increase because of the root delusions, they are (called) auxiliary delusions.

Hatred is strong anger approaching violence. With resentment you stubbornly hold a grudge and seek revenge. Concealment of non-virtues is the devious attitude of attempting to hide from others the fact that you have committed a specific black karmic action. Outrage is the residue of a strong feeling of anger expressing itself in your use of harsh and abusive language.

With jealousy you cannot bear to see or hear about the good qualities of others. With miserliness you always want your possessions to last and increase. Concealment of shortcomings is the ambitious and dishonest attitude of trying to gain advantage by hiding your faults from others. With pretentiousness you claim to possess qualities and abilities you do not have.

Smugness is an attitude of haughty snobbery and conceit. With it you are filled with self-importance, always criticizing and finding fault with everything you meet. Merciless cruelty is a total lack of feeling or consideration for others. It causes you to treat others as if they were inanimate objects, often with great maliciousness. With shamelessness you are concerned about the consequences of your actions on yourself. With inconsideration you are similarly unconcerned about the consequences to others.

Muddleheadedness or foggy-mindedness is a state of mind in which your body feels weak and your mind works slowly. You are overcome with sluggishness and do not wish to do anything. With mental agitation your mind, compelled by attachment or desire, loses its hold on an object of cognition and is drawn uncontrollably to another one, either virtuous or non-virtuous. Disrespect is your disinclination to virtue, often based on laziness. Laziness is the attraction you have to relatively easy and generally non-virtuous activities.

With recklessness, negligence, carelessness or indiscretion you do not guard your actions to see whether they are virtuous or non-virtuous. It is the opposite of care and awareness. Forgetfulness prevents you from remembering what you once knew. With inattentiveness you intentionally seek mental distractions and spend your time daydreaming. Mental wandering is an attitude of restlessness motivated by any of the three poisons of desire, hostility or closed-mindedness. With this your mind is never steady, but always flitting from one object to the next.

As all these attitudes derive from the six root delusions they are known as auxiliary.

Sleep, regret, coarse and subtle discernment are the four changeable secondary mental factors. They change over and again to become virtuous, non-virtuous or unspecified in accordance with either your motivation or (what type of mind) they are concomitant with.

Sleep is a state of total sensory darkness in which your five types of sensory consciousness cease to function, leaving you only with mental cognition. Depending on your state of mind when falling asleep, such cognition will be virtuous, non-virtuous or what has been unspecified by Buddha to be either.

Regret is an attitude preventing mental bliss or satisfaction. Feeling badly about non-virtuous deeds you have committed in the past is virtuous. On the other hand to feel this way about your virtuous acts is non-virtuous since it prevents you from enjoying their fruits.

With coarse discernment you seek a rough understanding of an object of cognition with little analysis of particulars. With subtle discernment you seek a more precise understanding of it. How these secondary mental factors are classified depends on whether the object you choose to understand is virtuous and so forth.

Thus every cognition you have entails secondary mental factors. Some are always present, neither beneficial nor detrimental. Some are virtuous, others are not. By learning to discern which factors accompany your perceptions, inferences and so forth, you can make all your cognitions virtuous as well as valid.

15

Other Buddhist Theories

The (tenets of the) Sautrāntka division of the Mādyamika-Svātantrikas, the Mādyamika-Prāsaṅgikas and the Vaibāṣikas assert (only) three types of bare perception: sensory, mental and yogic. They do not accept the bare perception of awareness of consciousness. However, those of the Sautrāntikas, Cittamātrins and the Yogācāra division of the Mādhyamika-Svātantrikas insist on four types of bare perception: sensory, mental, that of awareness of consciousness and yogic.

The purpose of Buddha's teaching many different theories, such as those concerning the mind and how it knows things, is to help lead sentient beings to Enlightenment. Although such explanations may seem contradictory at first, upon deeper contemplation it becomes evident that they are not. First Buddha teaches a very rough, general description of how the mind works. When you have understood this much, then you are ready to comprehend further refinements and more precise descriptions.

If you wish to define something specifically and exactly, you use a double negative—it is what is left over after you have excluded everything it is not. The more precise an explanation of the mind, then, the more you know what it is not. The more you know what it is not, the finer your understandings of what it is. Therefore it is important to train yourself through the graded explanation of Buddha's different schools of theories, from the Hīnayāna ones of the Vaibhāṣikas and Sautrāntikas through the Mahāyāna ones culminating in the Mādyamika-Prāsaṅgikas, in order to attain Enlightenment for the sake of benefiting all sentient beings.

One of the major points upon which further refinements are given is awareness of consciousness—how it is that you experience what you do and later can remember it. A more precise understanding of the actual way in which all things exist leads to a finer appreciation of what it means for something to be an external object, or something in the past. Thus there are further discussions of objective conditions for bare perception, what is subsequent cognition, what are the natures of objective and metaphysical entities, what is appearance, reality, deceptive cognition, ultimate and relative truths, direct and indirect apprehensions, and so forth.

Another topic discussed is how karmic seeds of instinct for future cognition are transmitted from lifetime to lifetime. In this context foundation consciousness, the mindstream and the process of mental labelling are examined further. A finer understanding of Identitylessness leads to further refinements concerning bare yogic perception, who has it and at what stage of development.

By following a path of learning how the mind works validly, you can come to understand how the omniscient mind of a Buddha knows everything. By hearing this, contemplating and meditating upon it, you can develop such an omniscient mind yourself. Such training, then, is part of the pathway to Enlightenment.

Because I feared this work might become too long, I have presented, more or less, only some basic lists. For specific examples of what has been defined, meanings to be understood and so on, please consult the general works (on Dharmakīrti's *A Commentary to [Dignāga's 'Compendium of] Validities'*), as well as *A Filigree of (Valid) Lines of Reasoning* (by His Holiness the First Dalai Lama) and so forth.

In order to (show) the hair-splitting differences concerning ways of knowing, which entail what should be accepted and rejected by those of subtle and aspiring intelligence, this brief compendium of jingles on ways of knowing has been compiled by someone named Lo-zang. By virtue of the effort made in this work may the eyes of all beings be opened to see what is correct or defective. By following to its conclusion this excellent and unmistaken path, may everyone quickly attain the Omniscence of Buddhahood.